D1568148

Linda Leigh Paul

lakeside living

WATERFRONT HOUSES, COTTAGES, AND
CABINS OF THE GREAT LAKES

UNIVERSE

Icicles cover the tree branches.

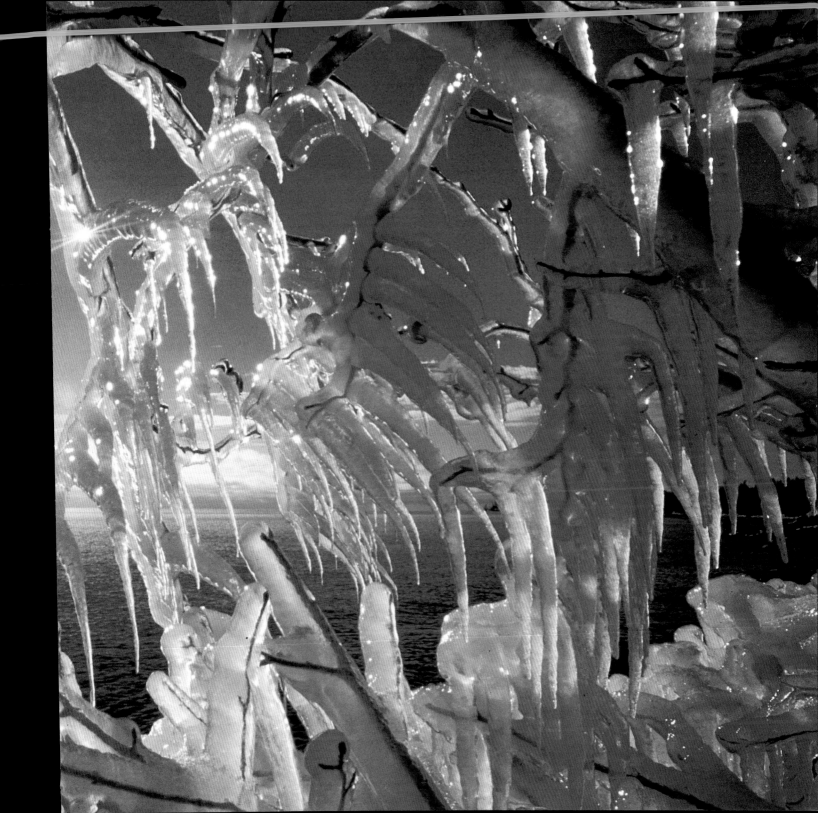

First published in the United States of America in 2007
by UNIVERSE PUBLISHING
A Division of Rizzoli International Publications Inc.
300 Park Avenue South
New York, NY 10010
www.rizzoliusa.com

2006 2007 2008/ 10 9 8 7 6 5 4 3 2 1

Distributed to the U.S. trade by Random House, New York

DESIGN: Amelia Costigan

Printed in China

ISBN: 0-7893-1532-7
ISBN: 13: 978-7893-1532-8

LIBRARY OF CONGRESS CONTROL NUMBER: 2006906710

ABOVE: *Heavy fog whitens spider webs that cover the needles of pine branches on Lake Superior's Stockton Island in Wisconsin.*

contents

A section of landscaped waterfall in an abandoned quarry gently cascades over the rocks on a crisp autumn morning, with mist rising from the water.

Trees line the shore of Lake Superior.

*The Indiana Dunes
National Lakeshore on
Lake Michigan, Indiana.*

introduction

*"Each day a new situation, chosen at pleasure; a neat, commodious house, built
and furnished with all necessaries, in less than a quarter of an hour, with a pavement of
flowers springing up on a carpet of the most beautiful green; on all sides simple
and natural beauties, unadulterated and inimitable by any art." [1]*

—CHARLEVOIX
Description of a voyage to the
Detroit of Lake Erie, 1721

ARCHITECTURE IS AS ORGANIC TO THE GREAT LAKES REGION as are morels, or trout. The
region is vast, stippled by lakes uncountable and rivers that bind marshes and canals to each
other. The water is fresh and clear enough to swim in with your eyes open. It may not seem that
that would be remarkable, but try it in a swimming pool or an ocean. Architecture in the region
is the process of building with one's eyes open. It is not for show; it is for real. It rises from
under fallen leaves, persists in the sandy dunes, and hangs over the edges of quarries and docks.
A discussion about architecture in the Great Lakes region is a joy. Excerpts from a recent conversation with a new acquaintance follows:

DAVID: It would be difficult to talk about design in the Midwest without talking about Cranbrook, the broad spectrum of design instruction there, and the support for innovation and rigorous discovery. Both Eliel Saarinen and his son Eero were deeply involved in Cranbrook: Eliel became president of the academy. It was Eliel who was responsible for attracting Eero and Charles Eames as teachers. Intrinsic to the school is an ethic of "Making," which is evident in its approach to crafts-manship and furniture design. This, too, is in line with the Bauhaus ethic of Making, where artist, craftsman, and architect work together. Cranbrook, however, has a more humanist variety, in harmony with the Saarinen Scandinavian influence, that is much more colorful and much more sexy. Mies and Gropius came out of the Bauhaus form-follows-function hard line—a design transfer that went both ways in the 1920s and 30s. European modernists were so fascinated by American grain elevators and warehouses. Mies's influence on Chicago was greatest in the fifties, sixties, seventies (eighties, nineties, and still continues. . .). I don't think it plays as much of a role in the architecture around the Great Lakes, except in the structural sense. For instance, Richard Meier's great white house, the Smith House in Harbor Springs, is widely seen as inspired by Le Corbusier. Maybe on the surface, but I think it is actually a Miesian vision at the core. Structural and brave. Wide open. Hell of a house to keep warm, I understand. If it were me, I'd buy sweaters. . .

Lake Superior Native American paintings depict life on land, on the water, and under the water.

LINDA: I am surprised that your first thought about Great Lakes architecture and design is of Cranbrook. I think of Frank Lloyd Wright as the pervasive influence of the region. By the time the Saarinen contributions of Beaux Arts *qua* Arts Nouveau aesthetic were emerging in the United States, Wright had already passed through the Prairie style—the Robie House, Wright's last Prairie house, was built in Chicago in 1908.

Native American pictographs along the shore of Lake Superior.

DAVID: Oh, you certainly couldn't breathe without the aura of Frank Lloyd Wright. He is the shining star and the enigma all rolled into one.

LINDA: . . . and one who finally gave us all a definition, an image-object, for the word "prairie." He wrote, "As a boy, I had learned to know the ground-plan of the region in every line and feature. For me now its elevation is the modeling of the hills, the weaving and fabric that clings to them, the look of it all in tender green or covered with snow or in the full glow of summer that bursts into the glorious blaze of autumn. I still feel myself as much a part of it as the trees and the birds and bees are, and the red barns." Wright had his early design influences, the shingle styles of the day, and [Louis] Sullivan's "organic architecture," which originated in nineteenth- century European theories of evolution and genius. The design kernel in the Great Lakes region unfolded in a conflation of sources, including an agricultural and

industrial utility, and immigrants infused with a heritage of European craftsmanship, who were eager to achieve success. Originally the Sheboygan Union Iron and Steel Foundry was purchased by John Michael Kohler, an Austrian immigrant, and produced cast iron and steel tools for farming. Kohler later developed casings for furniture factories, then expanded to garden furniture, settees, and urns. He had a great idea to improve his customers' quality of life when in circa 1883 he experimented with an application of a baked enamel coating on a horse trough/hog scalder and created the company's first bathtub. The early Kohler Company is a variation of what later emerged in the Bauhaus under Gropius as the *vorkurs,* a type of laboratory where success was measured by artists, craftsmen, and architects (often engineers) who worked together using form, color, and industrial products fused with practicality. Is this the basis of design in the region, a constitutional sensibility?

CLOCKWISE FROM UPPER LEFT: *The living room above the lake in the cottage interior. (2) The family and music area opens to the terrace. (3) A long, narrow, split-level guest bedroom. (4) The lower-level dining and game room lead to a terrace.*

What I am trying to work out is the adaptation from the farm vernacular to modern design and why the Great Lakes region so readily accepted modernism. Was it because their farming vernacular was the essence of a "form-follows-function" methodology?

DAVID: If that were strictly the case, Oklahoma, Kansas, and Nebraska would also be hotbeds of modernism. There is something else in the puzzle . . . but the expedience of design and the simple use of materials is definitely Prairie School, definitely agrarian based. I am reminded of my favorite Japanese period, the Shoin style, which also came out of taking the agrarian vernacular to a high art.

LINDA: Yes, the Katsura Palace is of that origin and period. It began as little more than a teahouse in a melon field and grew over time. The Shoin style began in the early seventeenth century, I believe, very simple, as the prince who was building it had few resources, and decorative and entertainment motifs had not yet entered the architectural vogue. Today, the palace is a treasure of Japanese architecture—"weathered but sturdy"—and the building still has most of the original wood that was used to build it. The simple design and floor plan were viewed by Walter Gropius and others as an early example of a quite modern concept.

DAVID: The presence of an abundance of good-quality wood and consequently, good craftsmen, does play a role. The Great Lakes basin built Chicago in white pine and oak, then built it again after the 1871 fire. Having that material and those

Frank Lloyd Wright's beloved "ground plan" of the rolling hills of Wisconsin from his living room at Taliesin, Spring Green, Wisconsin.

ABOVE: *A typical French agricultural prairie house in the Illinois Country, ca. 1830. The style is a predecessor to the Roi-Porlier-Tank cottage of Green Bay, Wisconsin, which is considered to be the oldest house in the state.*

BELOW: *Swans in a pond at Katsura Palace, in Kyoto, Japan. The palace grew out of the Shoin style, which itself began in the agrarian vernacular of the early seventeenth century.*

craftsmen around as a baseline resource played a role and raised design expectations. Yes, mass production, the auto industry, and even leisure have contributed to the mix. Who could enjoy the lake without a boat? Sometimes those boats are works of art in themselves.

LINDA: Indeed. Boats have it. I grew up on Lake Huron and enjoyed the sailboat regattas and the classic inboards. I think everyone, from architect and carpenter on, envies the boat builder. What could be better than virtuous design: graceful, tight, and sturdy construction? Boats conquer; the simpler they are, the better, from my perspective. You did touch on a point, though, one I've been thinking about as connected to the great Midwest architects. Great Lakes vernacular architecture contributed in exactly the same way as the evolution of the Shoin style: the agrarian foundations for a zen of less is more, a fundamental type of architecture that eventually expanded by adding features. Those features, compartments, and niches were primarily for the purpose of displaying objects. The Shoin style added display and entertainment features to the architecture as social styles changed. The same is true of the Great Lakes vernacular; the horse trough became the enamel-coated bathtub, which then needed a place or a room of its own in the simple farmhouse. That is not to say that there were not luxurious homes in the region. There was such a large variety—critics in the 1930s described the region as having a "battle of the styles."[2] Those weren't indigenous; they did not abide by the inherent forces of topography, climate, and adaptation. In spite of the early clash of styles, Great Lakes architecture is now the geographical *locus* of modern architecture in the western hemisphere. What developed here could not have happened elsewhere—it is a product of its locality and the convergence of influences brought upon it in that locale. It would be difficult to attempt to transplant these designs with success. They are not only contingent upon the climatic, architectural, and aesthetic influences, but upon the material resources—stone and wood, and following that, steel and glass. We may find displaced versions of them elsewhere, but this is where they belong, with the morels and the fish.

notes

1 Jerry Dennis. *The Living Great Lakes: Searching for the Heart of the Inland Seas* (New York: Thomas Dunne Books, 2003), 87.

2 Rexford Newcomb, *Outlines of the History of Architecture IV* (New York, 1939), 126.

Alden Dow's 1934 house is an example of the Japanese simplicity, organic and agrarian architectural forms that had an influence at Taliesin in the 1920s.

country home

ARCHITECT: Kathryn Quinn

PHOTOGRAPHERS: Minh + Wass Photography

At 3,400 square feet, this wonderful vacation home sits above the lake looking like a very charming country cottage. Its size is marvelously contained through the insights of its architect, Kathryn Quinn, who understood that her clients were seeking a place that would capture the spirit of the wife's grandmother's own vacation cottage. The owners, a professional couple from Chicago, desired a classic home with a sense of an era past, of time standing still and a place where instinctive and emotional actions are enough.

The home is tucked into its landscape where it seems to have grown. Large, high-rising stone chimneys along with cedar-clad exterior walls and roofs are used extensively to offset paned windows and steeply pitched, multidirectional rooflines. Outside, above the great blue undulating lake, the property is kept in constant motion with flower and vegetable gardens growing in raised beds, pathways curling around trellises heavy with trained wisteria, surrounded by hydrangea globes, begonias, honeysuckle, picket fences and with an eyebrow window above the screened sun porch peeking out over the gardens.

RIGHT AND OPPOSITE:
The subtle colors of the
unpolished river rock
dominate the great
room from the floor
to the open-raftered
ceiling to the fireplace
and chimney front.

The natural materials add to the rustic character, as does painted wood. To see the lake from the interior of the house, the architect was careful to select individual and distinct views and frame each with more than one hundred windows. "Western sun is, of course, the most intense form of natural light," claims Quinn. As a way of preserving fabrics and furnishings, Kathryn shielded the west-facing windows, and resolved the possibility of overheated rooms by adding a series of covered porches designed so that the summer light enters at a low angle, but the summer heat is high and deflected. Quinn stained the porch ceilings an opaque white to direct the low diffused light into the interior spaces. The combination living, dining, and family rooms are just off the kitchen, a gathering place that family and friends call the "Big" room. It flows three ways, to the kitchen, to the lovely screened porch, and to the bedroom wing and study beyond.

Kathryn's clients feel right at home in their updated grandmother's cottage. They now spend as much time there as possible—to simplify.

RIGHT: *The weathered country home and well-tended garden sit high above Lake Michigan.*

OVERLEAF LEFT: *The simplicity of the cottage is sustained in the great room by the use of a large hanging candelabra.*

OVERLEAF RIGHT: *The country kitchen features a marble-topped vintage cabinet as the island and period features from the 1920s, such as simple cabinets and platform risers under the stove and bread table.*

ABOVE LEFT: *A second-floor child's room fills with natural light. Painted pine bead-board wainscoting creates the cozy cottage room.*

ABOVE RIGHT: *The second-floor master bedroom features one of the cottage's three stone fireplaces. French doors at the lake end of the suite open onto a porch with perfect views.*

LEFT: *Trundle-bed furniture and milk-glass fixtures are crisp, simple furnishings.*

OPPOSITE: *Skylights and paned windows surround the tub in the master bath.*

RIGHT: *A waterfall cascades over layered rocks into a flooded quarry.*

OPPOSITE: *The view from the front lawn of two of the three houses with a connecting atrium and curved corridors with glazed French doors.*

stonemill

ARCHITECT: Les Andrew

PHOTOGRAPHER: Les Andrew

STONEMILL IS A REMOTE FORTY-FOUR-ACRE SITE OF FORESTED AND QUARRIED LAND. Two abandoned stone quarries are on the property, both of which have been flooded and so dictated the appropriate entrance to the property, as well as pinpointed the location for the house itself. The route curved around the flooded north quarry. It was decided that the house should be designed in three sections—north, middle, and south—which would be linked to each other by glazed atria, curved to wrap around the contours of the water-filled quarry. The views from the north house are across the quarry to the west, to take advantage of the setting sun. The home is a retreat for an extended family and guests who are spread around the world. The north house is the parents' domain; the middle house is the main guest quarters; and the south house is for the grown children and their families. Each house provides independent living with kitchen, dining, and living spaces, with a broad summer deck linking the three houses, each with distinctive viewing areas.

LEFT: *One of two atria featuring in-floor radiant heating. The rooms were designed with sliding and folding glass walls on both sides to transform them into outdoor spaces in summer weather.*

ABOVE RIGHT: *A curved corridor links the south house to the billiards and cards room in the middle house. The corridor features a brick wall on the forest side and French doors facing the quarry side.*

The owners wanted the appearance of Stonemill to be typical of the indigenous Niagara area styling of wood siding, double-hung windows, and cedar shingle roofs. Also, they wanted the buildings to be sited with a dedicated sense of stewardship for their land of biodiversity. Landscape architect and naturalist David Tomlinson prepared a plan that took into consideration the nesting sites for migrating butterflies, habitat safety for small animals, and provisions for nesting or migrating birds, including bird houses. Boreal forest trees and shrubs were identified and new specimens were planted to reinforce damaged areas. The wide-open spaces were gently contoured and planted with wild flower seed mix growing to meet the edge of the quarry. The water in the quarry is fed by underground aquifers, and the creation of one quite distinctive feature, a fourteen-foot cantilevered waterfall, provides a lovely visual and soothing sounds as Stonemill's musical backdrop to nature. The water over the falls has caused the rock bass and the painted and snapping turtles to flourish. On the bank of the flooded quarry the owners planted more than fifty thousand bulbs for a happy carpet of color and the first sign of spring after the long Canada winter.

ABOVE: *The billiards room re-creates a space from a former home in Niagara-on-the-Lake. The wainscot paneling and all interior millwork features are in dark-stained mahogany. The chesterfield is on a raised platform to allow better viewing for spectators.*

LEFT: *Fourteen thousand gallons of water an hour pour over the newly created waterfalls. This view is of a section that drops approximately fourteen feet to the water.*

OPPOSITE: *The children's paddling area and beach are in the foreground with the gazebo on the quarry edge.*

ABOVE: *The sitting room in the middle house has a view of the gazebo, flooded quarry, and waterfall.*

RIGHT: *The guest bedroom in the north house is warmed by the fireplace and filled with light.*

LEFT: *Each of the house sections at Stonemill has a lantern cupola. The middle house, shown here, has a seventy-two-inch-wide chandelier. This sitting area at the top of the stairs is equipped with wireless and hard-wired Internet connections.*

ABOVE: *The north house shower, with benches and multiple shower and steam heads, offers great views of the woods.*

summer camp

ARCHITECT: Margaret I. McCurry
Project Manager, Susan O'Brien

PHOTOGRAPHER: Hedrich Blessing

OPPOSITE: *The open porch of the summer camp imparts a sense of well-being and a joyful time to come for its family and visitors. The forest-green-stained clapboard exterior is designed to eventually blend flaw-lessly into its location. A lower section on the left provides a place for recreational equip-ment and a path to the beach.*

SETTLED INTO THE CREST OF A FORESTED DUNE that slopes toward the water's edge on the southern shore of Lake Superior, this summer retreat was designed for a Detroit couple and their three teenage children. The house sits high on the property, as close to the shoreline as is permitted by the Department of National Resources. In fact, the footprint of the design was staked out by the DNR and is contained within slopes having an angle of repose no greater than twenty-five degrees.

The camp interior is designed as a large gathering space that occupies two stories and con-tributes to the habits and necessities of a close-knit family. The focal point is a towering two-and-a-half-story stone fireplace that separates and defines first-floor areas as it ascends through the vaulted interior. The main rooms of the camp are spread along the northern face of the house toward the lake, while the smaller rooms are incrementally "stepped" back, according to

BELOW: *Dining is framed in the simplicity of furnishings and an ever-present outdoors.*

OPPOSITE: *Built-in cabinets neatly define interior spaces on the main level.*

the stringent DNR boundaries. The smallest step back is a stair tower, and its landing serves as a lookout that floods the foyer with sunlight from the south. A continuous cantilevered balcony extends to the second-level bedrooms, providing a full view of the activities below.

The structure is clad in clapboard, stained a practical forest green so that it will eventually settle seamlessly into its location. The red color of the asphalt shingles was chosen to accentuate the casual nature of the camp.

RIGHT: *The second-floor balcony wraps around the great room and the river rock chimney.*

OPPOSITE: *The massive fireplace in the center of the central gathering space is surrounded by the other rooms in the camp and the second-floor rooms off the balcony.*

baer lodge

OWNERS: Tom and Michele Baer

ARCHITECT: Douglas Kozel

PHOTOGRAPHER: Douglas Kozel

THIS HOME IN NORTHERN WISCONSIN, amid days of cooling air and the scent of a freshwater lake nearby, is a collaboration between the owner and the architect that has been in progress for over a decade. What began as a pair of run-down cottages is being transformed into a collection of lively structures, now numbering four or five, both new and restored, and with more on the way. This is a remote part of Wisconsin, forgotten for decades after the treasure of its timber had been decimated. A few stalwart outdoorsmen would occasionally trek into the area, until finally it has reemerged as a pristine landscape, showing nothing of its spoiled past.

The first project was a renovation of an old boathouse. It was anchored to the land and extended a little over the water. The setting was too beautiful, however, to let an opportunity pass for a restoration befitting a cottage on a placid lake shore. The boathouse below, now clad in river rock, supports an upper dwelling of rustic character. The living quarters are surrounded by a strolling deck with rails of small branches in the Adirondack stick style. The interior is designed around a massive river rock fireplace and chimney, which carefully delineate the dining from the living area. The windows in the front of the cottage provide views of the water in a 180-degree setting. The stone chimney towers up the upper-level sleeping loft and through the roof. The sloping roof, with its large eyebrow windows, seems to wink at the passing boats as they return after a busy day on the water. The boathouse has an extraordinary relationship with the lake; visual, aural, and olfactory senses combine the coniferous aroma of the forest floor, the crystal scents of the freshwater lake, and the oils of the wood shingles—all of which conspire to create a Wisconsin-aroma recipe for northern woods health.

The owners' love of boats is obvious when the buildings in which to repair and house them are objects of desire themselves. A growing collection of meticulously crafted, small, vintage wooden boats called for such a place. The structure is of wood framing and sheathing materials selectively harvested from trees on the owner's property. The building is thirty-five by thirty-seven feet and is hunkered down due to a graceful upsweep of the roof, which shelters arched windows with views out into the trees. The undulating roof framing reflects the spirit of the construction of the wooden boats.

Among the crafted collection of buildings rises the lakeside residence for an extended family. The construction is a combination of load-bearing masonry, wood framing, and timber framing. All wood framing, including the timber columns, was harvested on the property. Most of the materials traveled no more than a few miles to reach the site. There is a two-story main hall with smaller rooms positioned at the corners, where each extends out toward the lake and the forest. The lodge itself was inspired by the great lodges of the National Parks, thus the commanding central hall at its heart. Local craftsmen created much of the project, and certain pieces of work were designed around their particular skills. The beauty of craft specificity can be seen in the ironwork, the timber columns, the Adirondack sticking, and the material finishes.

The central hall was designed for use as both a gathering place and a system of natural ventilation; the windows were positioned not only for the view, but for ventilation using convection and the clerestory windows placed above.

A collection of vintage "old hickory" furnishings from now-defunct resorts and an extensive collection of early-twentieth-century ceramic vases decorate and add a homey familiarity to this marvelous family lodge. The couple, who adores their collections and enjoys providing unique homes for them, is about to embark upon the creation of a collection of follies in the woods: an elevated tree walk with tree houses and nature lookouts. This is a family compound where everyone will be amused for a lifetime.

ABOVE: *A structure for the storage of vintage wooden boats was designed with an undulating roof to open up the walls to the surrounding landscape.*

LEFT: *Intricate cedar-sticking detailing sets off the window framing as a complement to the crafted boats inside.*

ABOVE: *This building for a collector houses an evolving accumulation of artifacts, toys, and machines.*

ABOVE RIGHT: *Open loft space on the upper floor is used for organization and display. Framing and furnishings are used to contribute to a sense of memory and discovery.*

OPPOSITE: *A restoration workshop has a collection of tools on the far wall. Ironwork and timber columns throughout the compound are the work of Wisconsin craftsmen.*

LEFT: *A large pavilion living space is surrounded by a wraparound deck where the setting sun can be viewed.*

BELOW: *The back of the river rock fireplace separates dining from living areas. A sleeping loft is above.*

OPPOSITE: *The stone and shingle boathouse with living quarters above is a sensory delight with the pleasures of lapping waters and gentle cross breezes from the lake.*

RIGHT: *The expansive lakeside veranda is designed for relaxation, cold drinks, and watching the ever-changing patterns of the lake.*

OPPOSITE: *A covered entrance to the main house is welcoming in the cottage style.*

harbor springs

OWNER: Rob Mossburg

ARCHITECT: Robert B. Sears

PHOTOGRAPHERS: Main House, Robert Sears
Guest House, David Speckman

THE MAIN HOUSE RISES ABOVE 950 FEET OF SANDY SHORELINE. The house is designed after the classic rambling cottages that were built in Northern Michigan at the turn of the twentieth century, as expressed by its gambrel roof, dormers, and many timeless architectural details. Four outdoor fireplaces create cozy vignettes on the 1,800 square feet of relaxing porches and verandas.

Nestled into the trees high on a bluff overlooking beautiful Lake Michigan is the Mossburg guest house. Below are the ever-changing patterns of light and shade on the lake surface and the sugar-sand beaches. Views from the porch offer daily, up-close sightings of eagles as they circle and soar at eye level. Occasionally one will dive to catch a large salmon from the lake. The porch runs the entire length of the house, with an outdoor fireplace and an enclosed sleeping porch for those who just can't spend a moment away from the wonder of wildlife.

ABOVE: *The guest cottage kitchen, pantry, and breakfast nook were designed for old-style comfort.*

The guest house is accessible only by a footpath. Hand-built stairs add to the seclusion and privacy. The owner, who serves on the board of the local land conservancy and is active in promoting smart growth efforts in Michigan, donated a large conservation easement adjacent to the guest house. The parcel will never be developed and will remain forever is this natural state. The house was designed to not disturb the bluff, and while three trees were removed, nearly all the native vegetation remains intact.

The exterior features a copper roof with a copper hatch opening to the sun deck. At 1,200 square feet, the interior includes a main-floor kitchen, dining, and living room, and a bedroom and bath. A handmade wooden staircase spirals from the family room to the upper master bedroom and bath, with views of the beach through the treetops. Designed to be a warm and cozy retreat in the winter, the house is quite casual and breezy in the summer. It is tucked into the trees to respect its surroundings in all seasons and holidays.

LEFT: *A cozy space in front of the fireplace. Circular stairs lead to second-floor guest rooms.*

BELOW: *The living space, wet bar, breakfast nook, and upper landing all have views of the lake.*

OVERLEAF: *The main house rises above 950 feet of Lake Michigan shoreline. It was designed in the style of classic, rambling cottages of the early twentieth century in Northern Michigan.*

LEFT: *The childrens' bunk room has an outdoor balcony.*

OPPOSITE: *An open-beamed ceiling and ribbon of windows make an airy, bright guest bedroom.*

ABOVE: *An irresistible sleeping porch is equipped with wind-guard curtains for guest comfort.*

traverse bay residence

ARCHITECT: Linda Searl

PROJECT ARCHITECT: Amy Graves

PHOTOGRAPHER: Bruce Van Inwegen

LOCATED ON GRAND TRAVERSE BAY, this residence is a collection of smaller buildings surrounding a main house to create a family compound.

The house is organized by three intersecting wings: the main living spaces are in the north-south wing; the bedroom wing is on the south; and the family room with kitchen wing is at the north side. The views are toward the bay and extend both east and north. The site drops ten feet along the front ridge, giving lower-level rooms views and access at the water level.

The house is described by its owner as modern but still representative of its geography. The materials are wood and stone, with ash and Douglas fir used in the interior. The roof is made of copper shingles. Smaller buildings include a workshop in which the owner works out structural product concepts in wood and aluminum. The garage includes an adjacent exercise room and a pool house.

The design of the house in three wings and its placement down a slope deemphasize the size of the structure. Each end of a building axis culminates in a destination, such as a large screened porch. The hallway leading to the porch is lowered and darkened so that the view at the end of it comes as something of a surprise. The gallery crossing the length of the house is tucked behind the large stone wall and provides a framed view of the bay. The upper gallery offers a means of moving from the master bedroom to the family room at the other end of that level. The bridge also provides a vantage point for observing the living spaces below and viewing the bay beyond.

OPPOSITE: *A lighted stone wall flanks the passageway to the porch with a surprising view.*

BELOW: *A crafted rectangular chandelier softly illuminates the dining room.*

RIGHT: *Graceful trusses enclose the two-story stone fireplace chimney, which divides the great room from the dining area.*

OPPOSITE: *Intricate timber trusses float above the music room and upper balconies.*

OVERLEAF LEFT: *The pool house and pools are protected by the vegetation and trees.*

OVERLEAF RIGHT: *A landscape of pergolas and covered walks leads to the pools.*

RIGHT: *The pergola is in the center of the garden.*

OPPOSITE: *Copper-clad barrel roofs unify the structures of simple, wooden forms, while creating alternating outdoor gardens and "play-rooms."*

walk gently

OWNERS: Greg and Kathy Plumb

ARCHITECT: Cheryl Fosdick

PHOTOGRAPHERS: Peter Kerze Photography
Jill Greer, Greer & Associates

THE POUNDING WATERS AND RHYTHMIC MOVEMENT OF THE WAVES of Lake Superior are felt on the bedrock at the shoreline. The pulsing engines of slow-passing, thousand-foot-long, oceangoing ore boats can be "heard" through the foundations of the house. In storms the prevailing winds often reach 100 mph, where this house, a cluster of connected and freestanding spaces built on a sloping rock shield of the lake's northern shore, inhales the wild, sometimes savage environment.

This is where Kathy and Greg Plumb wanted to retire and do what they love most: garden. They are avid gardeners, farmers, and foresters—people who will plant hundreds of trees and thousands of bulbs before they build on the stunning seventeen-acre site. The architect designed a farmstead—places for the individuals within, as well as spaces for them outside with their plantings. Like their plants, each client had particular needs for optimal growing

conditions. Kathy prefers morning light, full exposure to the perpetual nature of Lake Superior's dramatic forms, and proximity to the nearby creek. A writer and jewelry-maker, she chose to preserve an existing fishing shack and convert it into a studio perched at the edge of the rock shore. Greg's requirements led to a very different realm. He wanted to be elevated in a second-story space, removed from the activity of the house and, to a degree, from the lake. Having been raised on farms, Greg responds to protected views that include bits of outbuildings as a screen, a foil to an endless expanse and horizon. In the main house, his is the second-story corner, with a glimpse of the lake, but with a wing enclosure from the nearest structure.

The living room presents the design's more elemental exposure through a corner of floor-to-ceiling glass. The towering stone hearth and the wooden ceiling anchor and define space. Above, an open loft shares the lake view from a plush, sheltered sitting area. Kathy and Greg have lived in the Lake Superior farmstead for several years now. Their trees are beginning to mature, their plants are flourishing. They say their hardest work is done. They've come to like the winter best, when the outdoors is dormant, except for the big lake.

ABOVE: *The view from the bedroom window. The writer's/ artist's hut can be seen from the window of this room.*

OPPOSITE LEFT: *The artist's shed sits on the rugged rock shore of Lake Superior. The main house can be seen through the birch trees.*

ABOVE: *The trees and hut on the edge of the lake.*

LEFT: *Owning seventeen acres of lakefront property is an exacting existence in this rugged and wildly beautiful place.*

The living room presents the home's most raw exposure through the corner of floor-to-ceiling glass, where the oceanic scale of Lake Superior is experienced.

OPPOSITE: *The bridge is the path through the birches to the writer's hut on the lake's rocky shore.*

ABOVE: *A detail of the loft railing.*

harris residence

OWNERS: Joan Harris

ARCHITECT: Margaret I. McCurry

PHOTOGRAPHER: Hedrich Blessing

THE OWNERS DISCOVERED TWENTY-THREE ACRES OF A WOODED HEAVEN, including a consecution of ponds, a variety of views, and a wildlife habitat surrounding the Galien River in Harbor Country, Michigan. Their house was built along a sandy ridge in an area that reminds the owners of familiar Connecticut landscapes. This is a region of small family farms and vineyards, which influenced the design of this basilica- and barn-shaped residence. The most prominent feature is the use of clerestory windows on the first level, which perform a secondary use as monitors allowing the natural light to flood into the large, vaulted interior.

The interior spaces are arranged in a procession of rooms that are symmetrically positioned to progress along axes and cross axes. This placement allows continuous views and vistas throughout the interior from one end of the house to the other. French doors at the end of each axis also extend views into the landscape. Limestone floors are radiantly heated, and a ceiling of fabric panels in the great room, along with doubled drywall, improve the acoustics in the large, open interior.

The materials shift from metal on the exterior siding to concrete at the ends of the building. This is in reference to the changing materials used on eastern residential usage, while the industrial materials of corrugated steel, standing seam, and concrete, coupled with the barn-red accents, reinforce the Midwestern farm references.

OPPOSITE: *One-inch tiles were used on walls and in the shower for a crisp, uncluttered enclosure.*

ABOVE: *The master bedroom divides light and space with dozens of paned windows and doors.*

door county

ARCHITECT: John Eifler

PHOTOGRAPHER: William Kildow Photography

THE FAMILY HAS OWNED THE LAKEFRONT PARCEL IN DOOR COUNTY for more than fifty years. The parents and their five children spent summer vacations in this glorious place, living in a small two-bedroom wooden cottage until 2002, when the little cottage was destroyed by a fire. One of the sons and his wife took on the responsibility of replacing the old cottage with a new one and brought in Eifler & Associated. The firm had recently completed the owners' new home in a western Chicago suburb.

The plan for the new cottage was to have two wings connected by a central corridor and foyer. The cottage is arranged so that the owners and their guests can congregate in a large single space, comprised of the kitchen, dining and living rooms. The bedrooms are located in a separate wing and secluded from the rest of the house, allowing for tranquility and privacy. Each bedroom is provided with exterior doors to the terrace, for access to enjoyable views of the water and setting sun, and stargazing at night.

A variety of historical references and local materials are used in a very contemporary manner. Cedar, Douglas fir, and walnut were used for interior finishes and furnishings. Distinctive white dolomitic limestone from the nearby peninsula is represented in the white polished concrete floors. The showers were finished in matte glass tiles, reminiscent of the weathered glass found on the beach. Finally, the beautiful striated stone used throughout the house in fireplaces, interior and exterior walls comes from a nearby quarry.

All rooms are provided with exterior doors for direct access to the outdoor terraces and lake.

ABOVE: *This shared living space is paneled in ash-veneered plywood, offering an attractive contrast to the dark bamboo floors.*

BELOW: *The interior color palette of natural materials is intended to reinterpret the traditional rustic aesthetic of a weekend home.*

ABOVE: *A second-floor bedroom suite with fireplace and floor-to-ceiling glass doors and windows offers views of forest, lake, and terrace activity.*

BELOW: *A guest bedroom with fireplace faces the setting sun.*

LEFT: *Three private suites and a library are housed under the soaring roof plane. Roofs pitch downward over less important spaces.*

ABOVE: *A vision of a solitary moment at the end of the day.*

LEFT: *Custom shelving displays art and artifacts.*

OPPOSITE: *The heavily wooded site faces the lake on the south. The upper floor is designed as a private and self-contained week-end retreat for two people.*

greenlake cottage

ARCHITECT: James L. Nagle

PHOTOGRAPHER: Bruce Van Inwegen

WHEN MAKING A STATEMENT ABOUT MODESTY, context, and environmental requirements, it is important that the technical problems associated with the earlier particulars of modernism be resolved. The idea here was to construct a modest cottage and boathouse that were consistent with the maxim "small is beautiful." To pursue the two combined goals, the architects planned that the wood-frame pavilion be clad in a natural-finish clear cedar siding. The clerestory windows and twelve-foot rolling doors are framed in polished, sustainable mahogany. Wisconsin fieldstone from nearby quarries is integrated into the exterior walkways and retaining walls, and moves into the interior space as a framed and focused floor-to-ceiling fireplace and hearth, which divides the living space from a sleeping area. The nine-foot ceilings are varnished cedar; floors are cedar fir; doors are of lovely river birch.

The cottage was built on a south-facing, wooded, sloping site on the lake. The upper level enjoys views of the lake, and the lower level—for family, guests, and visitors—is a full story that opens directly onto the lake. A south-facing porch spans the entire south facade and is sheltered

The upper-level plan is a contemporary cottage design using a wood-framed granite fireplace in the living area. The fireplace divides the living area and master bedroom.

by a roof of cedar louvers, which allow protection from the hot summer sun and natural light in the winter days.

The cottage and its boathouse building follow the contours of an oak-covered hillside overlooking the lake waters. The boathouse aligns with the house, preserving the trees between the two structures. The two-story steel-and-wood-framed structure houses the upper-level entry to the living and dining rooms and the master bedroom. The lower-level walk contains the children's bedroom and a family activity area. This is a quiet, understated wood cottage that is clearly a modern building. The best part of the house combines indoor and outdoor terraces in a perfect balance of public and private spaces for informal living.

LEFT: *Kids' dormitory bunks are on the lower full-story level, which has full sunlight and opens onto the lake.*

ABOVE: *The kitchen and bar area on the east features high ribbon windows to allow morning light into the upper floor.*

OPPOSITE: *The spacious south-facing porches shade the facade with a roof of cedar sun louvers.*

ABOVE: *The cottage and boathouse were designed to allow green space in between and to minimize the impact of visual volume.*

RIGHT: *The architectural detailing of this whimsical nautical cottage retreat.*

OPPOSITE: *A casual entrance and foyer carry the lighthouse styling into the interior with a classic curved door to the tower staircase.*

bayfield carriage house

OWNERS: Jerry and Linda Johnson

ARCHITECT: Dan Nepp
Project Manager; John Enloe

PHOTOGRAPHER: Alex Steinberg

THE ONE DOMINANT FEATURE OF GREAT LAKES LIVING is the variety of lighthouses. The client of this architect was looking for a whimsical retreat that would capture the playful elements of a lighthouse that reflected the unique character of Bayfield in the Apostle Islands. The carriage house was to be used as temporary housing until the main house was built; then it would be a guest house.

The concept was to provide a form and spaces suggestive of a carriage house and a lighthouse. The goal was to inhabit an unconventional living space for the sense of getting away, but also to make it a very livable and appropriate place to be. Large-scale gables and recessed, arched windows allow the house to balance with the animated form of the tower itself, while creating dramatically framed views of the north woods and the lake.

The house was designed around the kitchen, where most of the living and eating take place in the vaulted space above the "carriage functions" below. The larger space is made more intimate by incorporating a banquette in the deep window recess and the curving canopy over the kitchen area. Intimacy and warmth are also created by the use of recycled Douglas fir paneling that wraps the entire room. The tower is not just an icon but is an integral and multifunctional part of the house. It contains the entry, the stair to the second floor, and the observation room, where built-in seating; cabinets and shelves for books, TV, and music; and dramatic views of the surrounding islands and lakes can be found.

The carriage house is across a circular driveway from where the main house will be located. Both are angled to take advantage of an existing opening in the trees and vista of Lake Superior. The tower and drive-through opening declare this house as not a typical house and will keep it from being confused with the future main house. Until then, all the fun is in the carriage house.

ABOVE: *The carriage lighthouse sits on a curved drive, angled toward an existing opening in the trees for a vista of the lake.*

OPPOSITE: *The sturdiness of a lighthouse greets visitors at the arched door and the porthole window.*

RIGHT: *Dark mahogany paneling and moldings enrich the interiors. The curved wall of the entrance from the foyer to the living room is echoed by the strong curvature of the bar and windows.*

LEFT: *The built-in window bench and curved overhead bead-board panel-ing recall captains' quarters at the aft of a tall ship.*

ABOVE: *The curvatures of polished wood supported by posts and columns confidently enfold the room. Large paned windows allow natural light to flood into the space.*

RIGHT: *The top of the tower is a sunroom and an observation room with built-in furniture. A glass portal in the floor peers down the center of the staircase.*

ABOVE LEFT: *A detail of wood paneling and trim molding used on the bar.*

ABOVE RIGHT: *The simple geometries of the tower stair as it reaches the floor of the observatory.*

LEFT: *Window grids on the ground level function as light monitors on the upper level to capture sunny days.*

OPPOSITE: *The exterior of the House of Five Gables showing the "anchor chimney" possessing order from the forest floor.*

house of five gables

ARCHITECT: Margaret I. McCurry

PROJECT MANAGER: Kim Carrol

PHOTOGRAPHER: Hedrich Blessing

PRACTICAL BUILDING MATERIALS AND DESIGN have always been a part of the Midwestern rural ethic. This modern version of the early farm structures and other vernacular architectural forms that populate the region uses some of those industrial materials and variations on others. Clad in vertical tongue-and-groove cedar siding, the "barns" are painted not the typical barn red, but a bright, pure red that simply says, "I'm not a slave to historical precedent. I'm just giving it an ironic nod."

Styled after a "push-me, pull-me" toy, two identical barn blocks slide symmetrically forward, bracketing the middle block that slides backward to permit maximum exterior exposures. Three gables roof each of the blocks while two other matching gables complete the cross axes. The axial plan creates vistas from inside to out and vice versa. The focal point of the three primary axes is a fireplace—a hearth, symbolic of home. The reverse view is into the hinterland.

The house is set on the crest of a sandy knoll amid five deeply wooded acres on the forested dunes that define Lake Michigan's eastern shore. The windows are set in transparent grids on the ground floor; on the upper level they become single monitors to capture the sunny days that are less frequent on the lee side of the Great Lakes. Inside the spare, luminous spaces, robust natural materials of riverbed rocks and hickory wood floors create a warm counterpoint to the cool, white walls. A sense of serenity is complete with the addition of minimalist furnishings.

Standing-seam galvanized-steel roofs shed the melting snow safely held by snow guards. Aluminum-clad windows and woven-wire stair rails and deck enclosures add to the industrial format. These taut compilations of archetypal barns are the culmination of a city dweller's dream: a tranquil forest retreat far from the maddening crowd.

LEFT: *Window grids on the ground level function as light monitors on the upper level to capture sunny days.*

OPPOSITE: *Minimalist furnishings give the interior a sense of serenity.*

RIGHT: *The luminous spaces coupled with hickory flooring and cool white walls offer a serene environment.*

OPPOSITE: *Robust river rock acts as an anchor in the airy room surrounded by forested land.*

OPPOSITE: *Volume and space here offer a composition of grace and strength in a contemplative setting.*

ABOVE: *The exterior of the House of Five Gables showing the "anchor chimney" possessing order from the forest floor.*

RIGHT: *Crossing the "gable to gable" bridge leads into the room of contemplative thoughts.*

OPPOSITE: *The cool, white walls are a striking counterpoint to the bright red exterior.*

dunewood retreat

ARCHITECT: James L. Nagle

PHOTOGRAPHER: Bruce Van Inwegen Photography

A FAMILY OF FIVE PICKED A STEEPLY SLOPING DUNE lost in the woods overlooking Lake Michigan for a house to be used as a vacation retreat and eventually a year-round home.

The Department of Natural Resources in Michigan passed a law stating that no building can be built within the lake area on a slope with an angle greater than 25 percent. The only relatively flat land was the top of a dune, which offered very good views but was a difficult construction site. By angling the road across the hill, the architects were able to develop a driveway with about a 12 percent slope. The house itself stretches across the crest of the hill. The contractor built the structure starting at the north end and "backed" out of the site.

The house has three floors. The main level contains a string of spaces that includes the living room, a dining area, and an open kitchen. All seem to exist in the treetops, including a deck and screened-in porch spaces. The childrens' quarters are below with a secondary entry. From the midlevel or main entry the circulation pattern flows behind the raised family kitchen, under a

bridge, and into the living room that overlooks the lake. The parents' quarters are above on the third level, accessible by a stairway that is set perpendicular to the circulation flow. The spacial sequence is asymmetrically dynamic.

The site, the family's needs, and a desire to experiment with volumes and spaces resulted in a beautifully unpredictable house connected to its environment and to nature.

RIGHT: *Kitchen and dining area floors are covered in saltillo tiles for ease and casual effect. The living room drops down for a cozy central conversation area and good views.*

RIGHT: *A hardwood-clad corridor leads to a casual living room with fireplace.*

OPPOSITE: *The lake just beyond the screened porch and upper balcony.*

Settled into the top
of the dune, the three
floors of the retreat
are dependent on the
string of spaces that
compose the main
level. They all seem to
exist in the treetops.

elevator bay house

OWNERS: Jason-Emery Groën and Jen Grasse

ARCHITECT: Jason-Emery Groën Design

PHOTOGRAPHER: Richard Martin

THE ELEVATOR BAY HOUSE IS INTENDED TO EXPRESS A SIGNIFICANT CHANGE in land use from former industrial purposes to sites for residential building along Lake Ontario. The experimentation with materials in this design is a reference to early heavy and medium industry along the Great Lakes shore and the direction toward more serene and valued residential use. The economy of the materials is also a way in which this design exerts is accessibility and its expression of new regional modernism.

At 1,300 square feet, the house is compact, with a diversity of purposes made possible through the creation of a spatial sequence. The southwest wall facing the lake and adjacent lands opens to the site and the endless sky. Large sliding panels in the main room provide an effective way to separate the more intimate and smaller areas of the kitchen and bedroom. Plywood panels and horizontal Douglas fir slats on battens wrap the "cottage" that is within the house and includes the kitchen, the main bedroom, and a spacious screened porch. The loft area, clad with galvanized sheet metal, encloses the main living area and studio.

ABOVE LEFT: *spatial sequencing in the compact house allowed spaces to be comfortable and livable.*

ABOVE RIGHT: *The kitchen is one of three spaces that are housed in the wooden cottage portion of the structure.*

The experimentation with materials connects the house and its history to the physicality of its location. The two main volumes are defined by steel cladding on the west (windward) side and allude to the industrial and agrarian landscape beyond. The softer, richer wood cottage detailing on the east (leeward) side refers to the nearby woods. The wood claddings, which wrap the house from the inside to the outside, sharply contrast with the galvanized steel and allow for a transition of the building scale from the open fields to the more intimate wooded area on the other side. The design clearly expresses the historical significance of its site while enveloping a compact dream—all within the city limits of Kingston, Ontario, on the edge of Lake Ontario.

The changing land-use policies allow new residences to make architectural references, through the use of materials, to the former early industrial uses along the Great Lakes.

The wood
"cottage" is wrapped
within the "house"
and refers to the nearby
woods.

OPPOSITE: *The simple beauty of dry-stack pillars enhances the timber posts and beams along the corners and porches of the cabin. The contrast of stone with the simplicity of a screened porch, trees, and the color of the lake nearby recalls a time of early cabins and camps.*

arrowpoint

ARCHITECT: David O'Brien Wagner

PHOTOGRAPHER: George Heinrich Photography

THE LONG, STONE-PILLARED FACADE of Arrowpoint cabin stretches parallel to the mirror shore of the lake. The interior living spaces are oriented to a southern exposure and run the full length of the porch, offering views of the lake, the water, and its wildlife.

This new cabin was built on the site of an old, nearly abandoned fisherman's shack. While other portions of the property were buildable and offered more dramatic overlooks to the lake, the decision to build on the location of the old shack prevented any additional destruction to the surrounding forest or lakeshore. Nothing on the property had to be changed to accommodate the new cabin. The styling and form of the cabin express a regionality that is rooted in the landscape. It was taken in part from the early cabins and lodges that dotted Minnesota's lake shores in the late nineteenth century through the first half of the twentieth century. The design strategies were developed in response to the hot and humid summers of the region, using simple, yet evocative forms with deep, low-pitched porches surrounding steeper gabled volumes. The porches were designed to be broad enough to keep out the summer sun while allowing cool lake

ABOVE LEFT: *The stair opposite the living room leads to bedrooms with views of the lake.*

MIDDLE: *Under the stair a shaker-style table offers amber jaune Mica lamplight in the small space.*

ABOVE RIGHT: *Below the sleeping loft is the dining table, where doors may be opened to catch any cross breezes to ventilate the house.*

breezes to filter underneath and circulate around the corners of the cabin and the pillars of the porch. The narrow floor plan of the house was also designed with the idea of natural ventilation and cross-ventilation of the rooms in mind. Lake breezes filter in through the French doors that face onto the water and flow outward through a bank of high windows, making the need for mechanical air-conditioning unnecessary, even during the hottest days of summer. In the winter, when cold northerly blizzards bear down from the Arctic, the cabin's low profile keeps it protected, cozy, and warm.

The owners, John and Donna, desired a simple approach for their cabin design, with inviting spaces that are closely connected to the out of doors. Their environmentally sensitive structure is built of durable, renewable, and recycled materials, and is nestled quietly among the trees, hugging low to the land, and with minimal visibility as viewed from the lake. The interior is a compact, multi-use living space, with a screened-in porch, a main-level bedroom, and a sleeping loft. Their dry-stacked stone and wood cabin is 1,800 square feet of rustic simplicity and beauty.

ABOVE: *Snug as can be in a cozy knotty pine room. The low ceiling and small windows make the room a secret hiding place to read and watch the lake.*

OPPOSITE: *The dry-stack fireplace with its simple timber mantle and stone hearth is the heart of the cabin experience.*

ABOVE: *Knotty pine open beams, floors, and wall cladding add a soft quality to the wood cabin for restful days.*

RIGHT: *The house tower provides a route to one of the few outdoor spaces, a rooftop terrace with a fireplace, and fabulous views of Lake Calhoun and the Minneapolis skyline.*

OPPOSITE: *Exterior terraces and towers are open to the beauty of Lake Calhoun.*

lake calhoun residence

OWNERS: Dave and Marian Peterson

ARCHITECT: Tom Ellison
Project Manager: Charlie Simmons

PHOTOGRAPHER: Peter Kerze Photography

THIS HOUSE IS LOCATED ON A SMALL CITY LOT adjacent to Lake Calhoun in the heart of Minneapolis. The lake has a walking path and bike trail that have become a well-known promenade. A parkway connects Lake Calhoun with Lake of the Isles and Lake Harriet. Almost circular in shape, the lake is ringed by houses that have a traditional architecture. Homeowners here have shown their respect for the traditional style, and it was with tradition in mind that the owners of this house, who have a more contemporary sensibility, led their architect to a design that was able to integrate the two styles.

The site played the dominant role in shaping the house. The main living level is set up one story

ABOVE: *Small windows are screened with fabric scrim or etched glass to maintain a sense of daylight and openness.*

OPPOSITE: *The soft color palette of the modern interiors and furnishings of the main living level present a relaxed urbanity.*

from the street, separating the living activities from a fairly active street. The height allows views of the lake and provides the family with some privacy. The main living level is open to the lake view and on the south to an additional open space. The backyard is designed as a terrace that is built upon the flat lower-level garage rooftop. A two-story stair-hallway curves along the length of the house with high, deep-set, narrow windows and a large skylight that captures east, south, and west light throughout the day.

Views and space are important on this urban lot, and they are accentuated. A lovely, asymmetrical front facade is created by the windows that wrap around the corner of the living room and the master suite. The tower provides access to the rooftop terrace, its fireplace, and a whirlpool, as well as to the skyline of Minneapolis and Lake Calhoun.

ABOVE: *The soft monochromatics of the foyer and stair as viewed from the dining room give a muted but zany accent to the light-filled levels above.*

OPPOSITE: *The spaciousness of the master bedroom with the attached terrace and expansive views of the lake complete the necessities of lake life.*

RIGHT: *The exterior of the carriage house is awash in vegetation and stone. The special nature of the carriage house as a retreat is its uncommon history for crafts and art.*

OPPOSITE: *The march of seven or eight silver fox knife holders across the mantel is a priceless glimpse of the collector's eye.*

old town carriage house

ARCHITECT: Stephen Wierzbowski
Project Architect: Sergio Guardia
John Mark Horton, Interior Designer

PHOTOGRAPHER: Doug Snowery

AN UNUSUAL COLLECTION OF SENSIBILITIES AND TALENTS converged in the renovation of a carriage house in Chicago's Old Town district. The then owner and interior designer of the 1881 house, John Mark Horton, was captivated by the work of the wildly talented Edgar Miller and the Paris-inspired Sol Kogen, both of whom were expelled from the Art Institute of Chicago in 1917. They were, nonetheless, stylistic innovators who worked on Chicago's nearby north side in the 1920s and 1930s. Although modernists, the two designers had an interest in bricolage, and they lovingly incorporated found objects into their designs: carved doors, diaphanous or colored glass, sculpture, and frescoes. Old copper tanks were made into hammered copper doors, while decorous tiles were worked into daedal mosaic paths.

Principal living spaces are on the second floor, where only big rooms matter. The contrast in scale and light is theatric.

A group of artists and architects was assembled to accomplish Horton's design. Stunning arrangements of stone and tile fragments were installed in the lower level foyer, on sills, thresholds, and hearths. New window openings were fitted with steel windows. Maple floors were installed to complement furniture and reflect light. Asymmetrical patterns of ribbed, clear, and sandblasted glass were designed to frame views of neighboring landmarks and the garden. Curved and rectilinear walls of white plaster were layered to create light coves, mantels, vanities, and banquette sofa platforms in the living room and study.

Conceived together as an urban villa, the principle living spaces are on the second floor, where only big rooms matter. The ground floor contains small spaces: an entry hall, a bedroom, a study, and a laundry. The contrast in scale and light is dramatic. The main living space of the house is tall, wide, and lit by large gridded windows. The result of three years of teamwork is a marvel of controlled idiosyncrasy. The elements create an atmosphere that is transporting. The simplicities and complexities are highly refined by the intentional omissions, of art hanging from the walls, for example, which would sacrifice the absolute pleasure of this villa for the city.

RIGHT: *Asymmetrical patterns of ribbed, clear, and sandblasted glass frame the views of the garden.*

OPPOSITE: *Furniture as still life regarding the simplicities and complexities of highly refined intentional omissions, or editing.*

LEFT: *The house was divided into public and private spaces to reduce the visual volume of the design. Monopoly house forms of varying sizes were attached to an appropriate neighbor.*

OPPOSITE: *The attractive properties of the individual structures increase the building's compatibility with the surrounding residences.*

eisenberg residence

OWNER: Gary and Barbara Eisenberg

ARCHITECT: Kenneth Neumann

PHOTOGRAPHER: Hedrich Blessing

A COUPLE WHO COLLECT EVERYTHING wanted to build a home that would be both a backdrop for their collections and a comfortable, relaxed environment for their family and friends. Both the clients and the architect shared a desire for a modern design. The community, however, is a conservative one and is predominantly populated by historic homes, many of an English Tudor design.

The house is large, and to reduce the building scale, it was divided into two parts: public and private. The two parts are connected by a diagonal, one-story "spine." With stunning results, the house was designed by the use of modular "monopoly" house forms of varying length and width, each slightly slipped from its adjacent partner. Two tall brick chimneys serve as bookends on the public facade of the house. An additional benefit of the irregularly positioned components is the creation of a number of important outdoor spaces for formal and informal entertaining.

The plan is modern—each space flowing into the next—altogether expressing the casual living style of the owners. Natural light is everywhere due to many skylights and windows, all of which offer a sensational view. The expanse of dramatic windows and the view from every room suggest an understated, quiet interior modestly subservient to its surrounding architecture and landscape. The neutral fabrics, however understated, exude a voluptuousness combining mohair, leather, and silk; deep, hand-rubbed mahogany in the dining room; cherry in the library; natural oak and sycamore in the master suite. Colors shift from subtle hues of cream to butter to celadon.

The building facades and roof planes of stained cedar are perforated by small windows and large, girded curtainwalls that are cut into the simple forms of the house, thus easing this modern house into its historic and much more traditional neighborhood.

LEFT: *Living, dining, and food preparation take place under a high-vaulted ceiling and patterned windows to admit light.*

OPPOSITE: *A casual corner in another of the monopoly shapes is part of a large, more ordered room.*

Walls slide and open from one module to the others, and the dining room is no exception. Here the room is also visible from the terrace.

RIGHT: *Stairways and hallways are staggered to meet the requirements of their individual modules. Unique interior spaces result in small galleries.*

OPPOSITE: *When the modules are separated the house becomes a compound with pathways and other common areas, such as the pool.*

RIGHT: *The simplicity and elegance of a few luster-glazed tiles appropriately placed are captivating.*

OPPOSITE: *This is a room to have friends gather near the fire with a glass of wine. Floor-to-vaulted-ceiling windows on the pool side and the exterior wall create a nearly transparent module.*

LEFT: *A view of the summer kitchen bridge, which floats above the summer dining patio.*

OPPOSITE: *A tucked-away mini bar, sauna, and master bath under an arched ceiling.*

fosdick retreat

OWNERS: Steve, Lisa, and Ian Fosdick

ARCHITECT: Cheryl Fosdick

PHOTOGRAPHERS: Don Wong, Roger Rask

THE LONG TRADITION OF NORTH WOODS CABIN CULTURE offered the owners of this suburban residence a way to celebrate the summer getaway feeling all year long. The house was designed for an active, outdoor-oriented couple and their young child. It is difficult to imagine how close this world of the woods is to the Twin Cities. Many people drive for hours to experience the joys of open-air cooking and eating; bunkhouses for kids; a sauna, privacy, and romance for the adults.

The five-acre site includes an area where two fingers of land approach and form a small, saddle-like depression between them. This topographical feature determined the siting of the house, which was built on the property line, where a microenvironment offered the greatest area of usable space. As always with cabin architecture, the land determines the design.

The owners wanted ample exposure to the woodland property and to the wildlife that lived underfoot and on the wing. The design solution, then, resulted in four distinct realms: the tree

Cheryl's designs are collections of connections and separations. Separate spaces are created around, under, and near other modules. Here a room is a connecting link between the tree house and the hill house. The outdoor space in between is a framed snowscape.

house in the forest canopy on one finger of land; the hill house that digs itself low into the under-story of the other; a see-through summer kitchen floating above the outdoor gathering space below; and a large flagstone patio under the summer kitchen bridge, extending into the commons.

This home restructures the interactions of family in the same ways that summer life does. The commons puts parents, children, and visitors—including grandparents—together to cook and eat in the glass-skinned floating bridge. In the summer, barbecues and picnics move to the other side of the transparent wall. The narrowness of the commons amplifies the greatness of the woods beyond, while the hearth of weathered-edged Wisconsin limestone draws the family inward as if around a campfire.

Kids have their own place—the tree house. The tower of this wing appeals to the little person's urge to be taller, see farther, and be bigger. Young Ian has a handrail his own size to aid his climb to the top. He has access to his own outdoor deck and plenty of dimensions for a young imagination to explore.

The house is also designed for love. A self-contained wing drops away from the commons and nestles under an arched ceiling. A tuck-away mini-bar, the sauna, and master bath are situated at the highest point of the arc. A few steps down one side is a corner fireplace and a window seat in the master bedroom. On the low side of the arc is a screened sleeping porch for hot summer nights.

The selection of materials unifies the home. The commons hearth, its floor, and the patio outside are made of limestone. Floor tiles in slate and flagstone combine perfectly with broad ten-inch-wide swaths of clear redwood on the horizontal span of the commons, unifying the tower and arc of the supporting wings. It is a house built for love.

RIGHT: *A gathering place for talk beside the fireplace, and also for dinners.*

OPPOSITE: *Cheryl Fosdick is a design pioneer. She loves gorgeous wood; she is a terrific listener and she is bold. Her forms never shrink back, but nestle into their sites.*

LEFT: *A few steps down from the sauna is a corner fireplace and window seat in the master bedroom.*

OPPOSITE: *Day beds in the guest rooms and fireplaces are perfect places for warming up while watching the snow come down.*

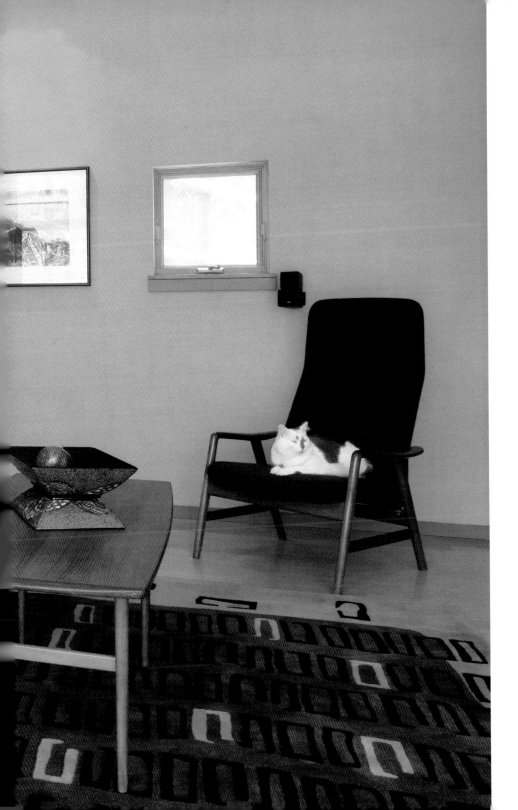

elliott retreat

OWNER: Dick and Karen Elliott

PHOTOGRAPHER: Art Curtis and Karen Walker

THE OWNERS ARE VERY CONSERVATION- AND ECOLOGICALLY-MINDED. Their house is hidden in the trees standing back from the lakeshore. In this home the owners' interests, tastes, and politics are freely expressed in the surroundings. The house is a workplace—evidence of that is everywhere. A variety of antiques and artifacts carry different motifs throughout the home and the grounds.

The rustic setting was discovered by the Elliotts, who both fell immediately in love with it. They designed and built the large cabin, taking down as few trees as possible. The curving branches on the trim of the house are the work of the owners, who animated the exterior by using freeform tracery designs around doors, windows, and at the peaks of roof overhangs.

Collections of museum-quality resort and rustic artifacts are housed in this handcrafted environment. Every individual item is an elegant example of a day gone by. A collection of fishing paraphernalia includes a copper creel, mounted bass, and framed illustrations of fish types.

Floors and walls are clad in Native American Indian rugs and weavings, as are chair backs. A small dining table is situated near French doors that open to the forested land on one side and the lake on the other. Period light fixtures, including Mica lamps, adorn each room. The warmth of candles in cast-off horn holders adds a touch of rustic authenticity.

The grounds share space for two additional small cabins and a boat dock. One cabin is a children's guest house; the other is used for boat and water equipment storage. The cabin camp is a tradition in itself, one that requires strength and a love of the lake. This camp is the culmination of both.

Rustic camps often are a collection of buildings that support a lively set of activities. This cabin houses gear for summer water activities.

LEFT: *The focus of the Elliotts' living room is the river stone fireplace and hearth. They brought a set of owl andirons to join pieces of Native American artifacts and antiques of model Chris Craft and other boats.*

ABOVE: *A serene place for a cool drink in a rustic corner of the porch.*

RIGHT: *The exterior view of the great room through cathedral glass and river rock framing the high window.*

OPPOSITE: *The approach to the main entry from the parking area. Large bent logs form an arch over the door.*

white fish chain of lakes

ARCHITECT: Katherine Hillbrand

PHOTOGRAPHER: Troy Thies

THIS LAKESIDE IS THE FORMER SITE OF A HISTORIC CABIN that had been cherished by the entire lakeside community, but that had fallen on hard times. The idea for the new cabin was that it, too, would be a gathering place for family and friends to relax and enjoy the outdoors. It was built with the texture and qualities that hearken to the great camps of the Adirondacks, and it was created to become a legacy for future generations.

The new camp was built with milled lumber, although it has the feeling of a sheltering log retreat from bygone years. The materials reflect and illuminate nature. The oversized stone piers of the cathedral window on the lakeside frame the lake between the majestic old pines. The light filters through the trees and gives the large and comfortable gathering room an aura of late afternoon serenity and peace. The gathering room is cradled among higher-than-usual cabinets, which house books, games, and music. The scale of the built-in cabinets creates the illusion of constricting the proportions of the room, making it ever more cozy. The fireplace

ABOVE: *The dining area features arched logs repeating from the main entrance. The dining table and chairs are made in the style of old hickory resort furniture.*

OPPOSITE: *A stickwork wood railing curves up the stairway and around the upper landing that overlooks the great room.*

anchors the corner of the room as a companion to the view and not in competition with it.

The dining room and kitchen are integral and tucked under the second-level bedrooms. The simple detailing in these rooms makes it comfortable for guests to show up for breakfast in their pajamas. The essential screened porch opens from the dining room and steps out to take its place among the fragrant old pines.

All bedrooms are on the second level found at the top of a gnarly, log-accented stair and a landing that looks over the gathering room. Each bedroom is tucked under the eaves. Dormers allow for cozy window seats in the children's rooms. The couple's bedroom has a small balcony that overlooks the lake.

The roofs are steeply pitched and cascade to the lower levels, thus reinforcing the reserved and submissive disposition of the new member of the community.

A small master bed-
room above a screened
porch has French
doors that open to
a small balcony with
a rustic, stickwork
railing. Setting suns
are the main attrac-
tion for this room.

ABOVE: *The new cabin was built to replace a cherished historic cabin that had fallen on hard times.*

OPPOSITE: *The new cabin was built with the hope that it too would become a gathering place for family, friends, and members of the community.*

wineman residence

OWNER: Jean D. Wineman

ARCHITECT: Terry Sargent

PHOTOGRAPHER: Jonathan Hillyer

LOCATED ON A RURAL FARM SITE, this residence evokes memories of the upper Midwest homestead where the architect grew up. The structure embodies the formal elements of a traditional farmhouse and barn, reinforced with the use of indigenous materials. Combining the use of cedar siding, pine framing, and local fieldstone with more traditional elements, the architect has demonstrated an inventive and sensitive approach to accommodating the needs of an active family of five.

Belying the simple rectangular interior layout, the exterior farmhouse shape houses the two-story bedroom wing. The main living spaces are enclosed within the traditional barn form. Exposed pine trusses create the main structural frame and are carried out to form the trusses that support the front porch roof and the carport. Side porches are covered by cantilevered roofs supported by cables that run through the interior of the house. The exterior is finished

in vertical fir siding in a reversed board and batten, a theme that is continued inside on walls and wood cabinetry.

Entry to the house is from the west facade of the farmhouse—a typical "five, four, and a door" composition of windows on the second level and windows that flank the entry door under the front porch. One follows the central east-west axis to the main living areas in the two-story barn. An open kitchen and dining area are to the north, and a sitting area is on the south. Along the central hall to the east are guest quarters. On the west end of the central hall are two bedrooms on either side. A winding stair leads to two additional bedrooms upstairs, each with access to balconies inside the barn that look onto the large vaulted space and the living areas below.

Two masonry fireplaces are made of local fieldstone and provide warmth to the large living area. The stonework rises through the second story, providing fireplaces for the bedrooms and culminating in stone chimneys rising from the rooftop. The main barn roof is lined with operable skylights to bring additional light to the living rooms and also to augment the natural ventilation. On the ground level, separating the kitchen and dining activities from the living room, a large elliptical opening in the floor slab is the basis of the central green atrium, supporting a ficus tree that has grown up into the open trusses of the second level.

BELOW: *The living area can be seen from either side of the house; in fact the glass walls at each end make it possible to see all the way through the vaulted atrium interior.*

OPPOSITE: *A bedroom on the main level with* en-suite *fireplace and granite fireplace surround.*

ABOVE: *A window detail of pine framing and shuttering on the bedroom wing building.*

LEFT: *Rural nirvana on a peaceful, cricket-croaking prairie night.*

RIGHT: *Rustic detailing of the front porch overlooking the river.*

st. croix rustic

OWNERS: Jared and Melinda Hoke

ARCHITECT: Katherine Hillbrand

PHOTOGRAPHER: Nick Gorski

THIS ORIGINAL "BARK-ON" LOG STRUCTURE was built as a woodsy hunting getaway in the early part of the twentieth century. A couple of additions were part of the way the cabin grew, near a small town on an idyllic river. The town is walking distance to the cabin and offers an old general store. People in the town feel a sort of pride of ownership for this quaint log structure. Katherine Hillbrand says, "everyone in the Midwest fantasizes about having such a place."

To accommodate the present owners, a musical family of four, the existing rooms were reconfigured. One bedroom became the kitchen and another became a music room, which opens to the great room. The old kitchen space has become a private study, and the front entry was moved to the space between the two gabled wings. A shingled addition was built on the north end of the house, which contains the family room, mudroom, and a small bath. Finally, two new bedrooms and bathrooms were added by excavating below the new and existing cabin.

Where once a trap door led to a small bedroom, three lower-level bedrooms are now approachable by the new stairway. The original and ruggedly beautiful stone foundation has become an exposed wall in the master bedroom, at the new stair, and in a small TV room. An arched doorway was cut into the stone wall at the couple's bedroom, and a "grotto" bathroom was added under the existing screened porch.

The relocated kitchen is adjacent to a newly constructed family room. A passage was cut through what was once an exterior log wall. New oak logs frame the opening. The bookcase to the side of the opening fills the space once occupied by an exterior window. A series of small, square windows was added to existing windows above the new kitchen center. The windows are lower than usual because of the extended roof eave, but they allow the cook a view down to the St. Croix River below.

The architect exposed the original bark-on log rafters and trusses in the great room. The dining area had originally been a porch. The screens have been replaced with a series of windows that wrap around the dining area. The furniture is from the owner's grandfather. Some of the pieces are quite historic, such as the wonderful sideboard, as well as the rugs still in use.

Exterior logs were cut to fit the new and existing structure by the architect's husband, Deane Hillbrand. The large corner oak log with bark still attached was cut from a property in northern Minnesota. It is still a puzzle to all how Deane was able to lift and fit that log into place, given that the roof and walls were already in place and that he had no tools other than a few "come-alongs." The log entry porch ties the new 2x framed addition to the old log frame. The cascading stair "spreads" the visual approach of the cabin to the visiting guest. Cascading rooflines allow this little cabin to hover with the history and mystery of its fine place.

LEFT: *Logs were cut to fit the new structure by the architect's husband.*

OPPOSITE: *The original rugged stone foundation of the lower level wall is exposed in the bedroom and at the new stair. An arched opening was cut in the bedroom wall and added a new "grotto" bath under the existing screen porch.*

ABOVE: *The newly constructed family room, with a doorway that was cut through a former exterior wall. The bookcase now fills a space once occupied by a window, and the kitchen is arranged between the great room and the family room.*

The great room for a musical family of four features bark-on log rafters and trusses overhead. Furnishings are family heirlooms.

LEFT: *The use of single, long-arched beams creates attractive spaces with complex and costly carpentry.*

OPPOSITE: *Soaring and curved rooflines mimic the curves of the surrounding dunes.*

cathead bay house

OWNERS: Jes Asmussen and Colleen Cooper

ARCHITECT: David T. Hanawalt

PHOTOGRAPHER: Peter Tata

"CATHEADS" ARE THE PROW OPENINGS FOR ANCHOR CHAINS. Cathead Bay has been a protected and safe harbor since the Great Lakes shipping of old. Sand Dune protection and environmental laws are restrictive along its beaches and yet provide the time to deeply study the site and arrive at a single creative solution. Two endangered species were known to inhabit areas of the beaches: the piping plover, a sand dune bird; and the pitchers thistle, a flowering shore plant. The architect located eleven of these rare plants with GPS.

The concept the architect arrived at for this house was to mimic the wind flow and the shapes of the dunes with the rooflines, which became very sculptural. The use of single, long-arched beams created attractive spaces with complex and costly carpentry. The heart of the house is a three-sided redstone/limestone fireplace. Four windows, two on the north and two on the south, are placed so that during the summer or winter solstice, a ray of sunlight is aligned to project toward the fireplace at sunrise or sunset. The sunlight stops at the fireplace—at the locus where the pure intellectual idea and the physical object of a building meet.

The house has a main area with dining space and an open living/master bedroom suite on the ground level. The second level contains an art and painting room, a studio, offices, and a guest suite with an outside deck. Jes has invented a way to make diamonds from carbon using microwaves and runs his own laboratory at Michigan State University. Colleen is a meeting facilitator able to make opposing sides of an issue understand the other side's positions.

The main entry to this house has a single aluminum column on the left side, while on the right is a tree. A branch of the tree is being "trained" to appear to support the right side of the entry.

LEFT: *Fishtown is a historic working fishing village.*

OPPOSITE: *Dormers and windows are important for those who watch the weather and wait for the fleets to return.*

fishtown cottage

OWNERS: The Carlson Family

ARCHITECT: David L. Hanawalt

PHOTOGRAPHER: Peter Tata

FISHTOWN IS A WORKING FISHING VILLAGE on a small Lake Michigan harbor. This is a historic harbor accustomed to lake-labor long-shoring resources such as lumber, iron, Northern Michigan agriculture, and, of course, fish. The most sought after is famous around the Great Lakes: whitefish, when smoked, is a world-class delicacy. The number of year-round residents has doubled in the last 150 years, but during the summer, this small place is a favorite for thousands of guests.

Fishtown is on the National Registry of Historic Places; it has been privately owned for many years by the Carlson family. Bill and Mark Carlson, two of three brothers, contacted the architect to work on one of the structures that was close to finally yielding to the elements. An old fishing shanty on a wharf, it was used to store fishing gear and to pack fish in ice for storage. David Hanawalt, the architect, was asked to re-create the structure using historic detailing and

BELOW: *Restored
or original, shanty
architecture built on
docks is a reminder
that all good places
to live grow at the
edge of a body of
water.*

scale. To begin, he carefully measured the existing structure and photographed the details of both the structure itself and other buildings in Fishtown.

Fishing shanty "architecture" has a typology of its own, as vernacular design, which became known through window and door configurations. The building was "taken down to the sticks" and built up again from the piles to the roof, replacing the entire structure within the original dimensions. Historically, the tall door and window in the dormer design were used for ice storage; horizontal boards were added from bottom to top as ice was added in the winter. In the heat of the summer, as the ice was used, the boards were peeled away top-down. Shingles and siding are aging as planned around a new main living space, a small kitchen and dining area, two bedrooms, and two baths. An outside deck looks out on Lake Michigan.

ABOVE: *Knotty pine and open beams are welcoming features after long days on the water.*

BELOW: *Upper rooms with window seats in dormer spaces and bedrooms with angles in the ceilings glow with knotty pine.*

muskoka boathouse

ARCHITECT: Brendan Smith

PHOTOGRAPHER: John de Visser

The Great Lakes region is extensive. It is the geography of large and small lakes and many rivers. It is also the home of the great recreational boats of the twentieth century. These boats were often housed in sturdy, articulated "houses" at the edge of a lake, some by their owners, others by well-known architects. The boathouse was for the purpose of accommodating the treasure of the water, the glistening craft of luxury, or the hand-varnished craft of the paddle. Each new boating acquisition was cause enough to have the boathouse modified as needed, generally on one level that was built slightly above the ordinary level of the lake. While the boathouse was a few feet from the shore, the main cottage and occasional guest cottages were to be found up the path, high on the bank and a distance away from the water.

This bulging point is on an island that juts into Lake Muskoka. The first known cabin on the site was built by a troupe of vagabond thespians who worked the summer theaters. The cabin was built for gatherings of discussions, entertainment, swimming, discovery, and amusement.

RIGHT ABOVE:
Painted bead-board paneling on walls and ceilings adds a nautical flavor to the sleeping area.

RIGHT BELOW:
Arched windows open to the sounds of the water birds, the lake, and the morning sun.

Guests camped in tents on the water's edge. Picnics, hikes, and long parties filled the days and afternoons.

Today, the east-facing location is home to a large cottage, guest house, and at the shore, a set of boathouses, with living quarters above the treasured boats. They are the reliquary of decades of family memories, for all the activity is generated in the boathouses. An early departure for a morning fishing trip is a good reason to pack and spend the night sleeping in the boathouse, listening to the waves splashing under the boats below as they roll onto the shore, ready for a very early day to come. After a long summer day of swimming, skiing, paddling, and a campfire cookout on an island in the lake, a restful night above the slow undulations of the boathouse couldn't be more heavenly.

BELOW: *The classic Muskoka Lake boathouse has architectural detail, flower boxes, garden furniture, and classic boats.*

LEFT: *The cottage view from the living room toward the lake.*

ABOVE: *The cottage is up the slope from the beach, where calmer activities take place on the porch.*

LEFT: *The architect designed windows with mahogany frames to modulate lake sounds in a variety of ways.*

OPPOSITE: *The heavy framed overhead lattice on the lakeside deck offers protection from the afternoon sun.*

wege residence

OWNERS: Anna and Jonathan Wege

ARCHITECT: David T. Hanawalt

PHOTOGRAPHER: Peter Tata

IMAGINE THAT THE SOUNDS MADE IN AND AROUND YOUR HOUSE were actually musical. Poet Johann Wolfgang von Goëthe in the early nineteenth century created one of architecture's most lasting metaphors by calling it "frozen music." Now, architect David Hanawalt, with the collaboration of acoustic artist Bill Close, has dared to unfreeze Goëthe's observations. Most architects with such insights about how to design and build are rarely willing to attempt this sort of full expression, depth, and dimension when given a project. Of course, there are houses that are so loaded with technology they can give a massage, but that isn't architecture.

David Hanawalt met Anna and Jonathan Wege at their vast and beautiful site, a stretch of pristine beach bordered by natural grasses and plenty of wildlife. Little compares to the sounds of the Great Lakes; their waves, wild winds, rain, woods, and wildlife are an environmental musical composition. As a windmill can receive, store, and transform environmental energy, so can a carefully designed house. Jonathan himself advises companies on improved environment practices, and Anna is an interior designer. They began planning their house, which was to become a receptacle of sounds for him with a modernist interior for her.

RIGHT: *As the upper rooms step forward, the exterior balcony becomes broader in width, creating a larger overhang.*

Sketching late one evening, over a glass of wine, David drew a design in which the house was a vessel for the beloved sounds, catching and transforming them. He began designing what would be first a musical instrument and second a beautiful lakeshore house. The Weges are a creative and enthusiastic couple with a willingness to build a lakeshore house to celebrate the pure joys of life, requiring David to use a degree of artistic and engineering faith to proceed with his conceptual design. Bill Close, an artist who had the rare experience and expertise of having created sonic art installations and performances in large spaces, was instantly absorbed into the idea of designing architecture as a site-specific musical instrument from the ground up.

The two harps in the main room are long-stringed and tuned to open string (A through G with two G strings), eight strings to each harp. When hands in gloves with rosin are pulled along the strings, a compression wave generates a harmonic frequency in the string tuned to the length. A string harp up and down the main stairwell also resonates within that space under the pyramid skylight. The tuning of that harp is dissonant and generated not by familiar musical scales, but by the geometry of the architecture and the stair. Walls treated with hidden epoxy, Calder pieces framed in glass, and large glass windows and baluster panels all contribute to the echoing resonance of the space and volume.

The entire effort was to create spaces that responded acoustically to their site, location, and use. That did not preclude visual interest; giving acoustics precedent in response to this site did not diminish the views. The architect designed windows with resonant mahogany frames to modulate lake sounds in a variety of ways, depending on which way the window was opened, vertically or horizontally. "I wanted the windows to be more like eardrums than eyeballs," said David.

Jonathan is an entrepreneur of sustainable energy products. The house is heated with a geothermal heat-exchanged forced-air and radiant system. A pond and garden behind the house is a thriving ecosystem from the open loop. A walking path of round stones and soft sand is planned to massage the feet. This is a temple for the senses.

OPPOSITE: *Bass strings are attached to the pyramid skylight, pass the window, then descend into the living room. Strings may be "played" from the second-floor landing.*

ABOVE: *Eight tuning pegs on "headboard" tighten and loosen the strings for a dissonant, unfamiliar scale. Heavy gloves and rosin are used to coax echoing resonances in the volume of space.*

OPPOSITE: *Gloves and rosin are at the ready to "play" the strings that run from the tuning pegs, along the rafter, toward the windows. Walls are treated with hidden epoxy and panels to contribute to the echoing resonances.*

ABOVE: *All spaces were designed to respond accoustically to their location and use.*

acknowledgments

I AM VERY GRATEFUL to the architects, historians, photographers, and homeowners who contributed to this work. My appreciation to Dr. Kathryn Eckert, Michigan architectural historian and author, is inestimable. Professor Gwendolyn Wright, architectural historian at Columbia University, offered enthusiastic insight in the development of the introductory text. I wish to thank Laura Rose Ashlee, publications and historical marker coordinator of the State Historic Preservation Office and the Michigan Historical Center; Daria Potts, director of the Alden B. Dow Archives at Alden B. Bow Home and Studio Organization; Chris Hudson of the AIA Minnesota; and Suzy Berschback, curator of the Grosse Pointe Historical Society. I am indebted to Margaret I. McCurry, FAIA, IIDA, ASID, for her contributions of time, material, and her unparalleled projects for publication. I wish to thank Dale Mulfinger, FAIA, for his help in tracking remote possibilities and to his firm for their wonderful designs. I wish to thank architect David Hanawalt for his perseverance and contributions to this book. Balthazar Korab of Balthazar Korab, Ltd., is one of the masters of the universe. His photography is a record of the excellence in architecture of the past half century, and his body of work is a treasure for us all. It has been my sincerest pleasure to work with him on this project. I offer my incalculable appreciation to you, Balthazar. Thank you.

I spent time writing and thinking about a perfect Great Lakes childhood. There are the families and friends to thank who share experiences and those whom I've not seen since childhood. I would like to thank Roland and Genevieve Galarneau, my parents, for bringing our family up on Lake Huron. Rick Galarneau and Dawna Galarneau Miller also share my everlasting love and gratitude for the joyful lake stories we tell every holiday. Kerry D. Hampton III knows more about Michigan than I will ever learn; his friendship is immeasurable. I want to thank the Piechowiak Family, Mary Ann McGarr, Nancy Harvey, Patty Barrett, Marilyn Carson, the Storey Family, Babe and Lady, and the others who were there to make our lake life memorable.

I am particularly grateful for the expertise and guidance of Alex Tart, editor at Rizzoli who is the best of the best. Her ability to balance, advocate, and produce takes tremendous skill and patience. Her support is greatly appreciated. Many thanks to designer Amelia Costigan for her excellent work. I wish to acknowledge Charles Miers, publisher of Rizzoli/Universe for his kind assistance and his vision. Thank you, Charles, most sincerely.

To the love of my life, Robert Paul, you are a very mysterious Minnesotan.